PRACTICAL DEFINITIONS

for the Working Professional

A Pocket Dictionary

KYLE HANLAN

1-10-100 rule:

This a principle of quality management that states that ascribes that the relationship between cost of prevention, cost of correction, and the cost of failure. Think of a widget that cost the company $1 to produce if there are no issues. It will cost the company $10 if there is an issue that caught before it leaves the company's building. It will cost the company $100 to correct if the issue is received by the customer.

5S:

A methodology that results in a workplace that is clean, uncluttered, safe, and well organized to help reduce waste and optimize productivity.

80/20 rule:

A principle that states that 80% of an organization's profits stem from 20% of the products.

Abstract:

A brief review of a report that summarizes major elements to enable a reader to understand the basic features of the report.

Acceptance Criteria:

The required conditions that must be met in order for the deliverables to be received.

Accepted Deliverable:

Products, results, or capabilities produced by an entity in order to meet the customer specific criteria.

Accountability:

Being answerable for actions and results of self or teams. Accepts consequences of actions.

Accuracy:

The average attempts that are in the center of the target but there is a lot of variability.

Acquiescence bias:

Also known as "yea-saying" or the friendliness bias, acquiescence bias occurs when a respondent demonstrates a tendency to agree with and be positive about whatever the moderator presents.

Acquired Resources:

Resources obtained for the specific purpose of completing project work, such as team members, facilities, equipment, materials, and/or supplies.

Acquisition:

Obtaining personnel and materiel resources from another element or organization.

Acquisition Lead Time (ALT):

The time interval between the initiation of solicitation/ contract negotiation and product production.

Action:

The process of doing something, typically to achieve an aim.

Action Research:

A disciplined process of inquiry conducted by and for those taking the action.

Active listening:

Technique of being activity engaged with the partner or audience.

Activity:

A distinct portion of an organization, such as a work group of division. In project management, this term represents the portion of work in a project.

Activity Attributes:

Multiple attributes associated with each scheduled portion of a project.

Activity Duration Estimates:

The quantitative assessments of the likely number of time that is required to complete a project.

Activity List:

A document that itemizes all activities (or entities) within an organization.

Activity-based Cost:

A method for assigning costs to activities and then reassigning activity costs products, customers and other cost objects.

Actual Cost:

The total amount of cost accrued throughout a project.

Actual Duration:

The calendar time between the actual start and finish dates.

Adaptive Life Cycle:

A program life cycle that is iterative or incremental.

Affinity Analysis:

A data analysis and data mining technique that discovers co-occurrence relationships among activities performed by (or recorded about) specific individuals or groups.

Agile:

The ability to create and respond to change.

Agreements:

Any document or communication that defines the intentions of a project, contract, or working relationship.

Alignment (behavioral):

The synchronization of verbal and nonverbal cues. For example, facial expressions or affect that match the words of the individual.

Allocation:

The indirect assignment personnel, costs, materiel, or other resources.

Alternative Analysis:

A technique used to evaluate identified options in order to select the options available to conduct work in a project.

American Production and Inventory Control Society (APICS):

An association for supply chain management and a not-for-profit international education organization. Considered to be the leading certification granting organization for supply chain management.

American Society for Quality (ASQ):

A professional organization centered around process & quality improvement. This organization is often referenced as the standard in Six Sigma certifications in the United States.

Analogous Estimating:

A technique for estimating the duration cost of an activity using historical data from similar activities.

Appraisal Costs:

The costs that are accrued through tests and quality inspections that ensure products and services meet customer expectations and regulatory requirements.

Armor Plate:

To bring software up to industrial strength by adding security and controls.

As-Is:

A description of the present state of the process or organization.

Assumption:

A variable in the planning process that is considered to be true without supporting evidence.

Assumption Log:

A project document used to record all assumptions and constraints.

Attitude:

A state of mind or feeling.

Attribute:

A specific value on a variable. For instance, the variable has binary property - cut or not cut, drilled or not drilled, action or no action.

Authentic Leader:

An approach to leadership that emphasizes building the leader's legitimacy through honest relationships with followers which value their input and are built on an ethical foundation.

Authenticity:

Fully aligned within self.

Authority:

The established placement of power and influence of a position or role within an organization.

Autonomy:

The degree of self-reliance and independence from the surrounding organization.

Back Ordering:

An item requisitioned by ordering activities that is not immediately available for issue but is recorded as a stock commitment for future issue.

Backwards Pass:

A critical path method for calculating the late start and late finish dates by working backward through the schedule model from the project end date.

Bar Chart:

A graphic display that presents categorical data with rectangular bars with heights or lengths proportional to the values.

Baseline:

A minimum or starting point used for comparisons.

Basic Ordering Agreement (BOA):

A written instrument of understanding negotiated between a procuring activity and a contractor that contains: (1) terms and clauses applying to future contracts (orders) between the parties during its term; (2) a description of supplies or services to be provided; and, (3) methods for pricing, issuing, and delivering future orders under the BOA.

Basic Value Imperative:

The idea that all organizations must provide unique, perceived, value added services and products in order to survive.

Basic Value Imperative:

The idea that all organizations must provide unique, perceived, value added services and products in order to survive.

Basis of Estimates:

Supporting documentation that outline the details used to establish the estimates of a program.

Behavior:

The actions of an individual or organization.

Behavioral Change Management (BCM):

A deliberate sequence of problem identification, organizational research, and behavioral interventions (impacts), all designed to align the organization's actions, attitudes, and desires around organizational goals.

Beliefs:

Mental acceptance or conviction in the validity of a person, concept, or value.

Benchmark:

BA standard against which performance or activity is compared and judged.

Benefits Management Plan:

The document that outlines the process of creating, optimizing, and sustaining program benefits.

Best Practice:

The practice(s) used to achieve superior performance.

Bid Documents:

All documents used to solicit information, quotation, or proposals from a seller.

Bidder Conference:

The meeting with a prospective seller prior to the proposal to ensure all vendors have a clear understanding of the procurement process.

Bill of Lading:

A detailed list of a shipment of goods in the form of a receipt given by the carrier to the person consigning the goods.

Black Belt:

A Six Sigma certification that demonstrates an individual's knowledge, skill, and ability to lead problem-solving projects. As well as train and coach project teams.

Blanket Order:

An agreement between a customer and the organization for a specific category of items or services (including training) with no definitive listing of items or quantities.

Blanket Purchase Agreement (BPA):

A method of acquiring a variety of goods and services from pre-approved venders. The federal buyer places orders through the BPA over the course of the year.

Bonded Warehouse:

A customs-controlled warehouse for the retention of imported goods until the duty owed is paid.

Bottom-Up Estimating:

A method of estimating program length and/or cost by aggregating the estimates of the lower level components of the work breakdown structure (WBS).

Boundary:

A border or limit between people and behaviors.

Budget:

The approved allocation of financial resources for an organization and/or program.

Budget at Completion (BAC):

The sum of all budgets established for the work to be performed.

Build to Order:

In this model the company begins assembly of the customer's order almost immediately upon receipt of the order.

Business Agile:

Ability of a business system to rapidly respond to change by adapting its initial stable configuration.

Business Area:

Any subset of the enterprise singled out for development or change activity.

Business Case:

A justification for a proposed project or undertaking on the basis of its expected commercial benefit.

Business case for change:

Presents a justification and process for changing something.

Business Function:

A collection of similar business activities that use common resources but that are otherwise unconnected.

Business Process:

The action taken to respond to a particular event, convert inputs into outputs, and produce particular results.

Business Process Redesign:

The replacement of an existing business process with a completely new or substantially redesigned one.

Business Relationship Redesign:

A redesign that expands the scope of business process redesign to include the processes of organizations external to the company.

Business Unit:

A type of organizational unit. It is a collection of work groups brought together for a particular business purpose.

Business Value:

The net quantifiable benefit derived from a business endeavor.

Business Work Group:

A collection of related resources brought together for a particular business purpose.

Buyer:

Any person who contracts to acquire an asset in return for some form of consideration.

Capability:

The skillsets, talents, and perspectives of people that are needed to complete/exceed the work.

Capacity:

Quantity of the capabilities required to complete/exceed the work.

Carnet:

A customs permit allowing a motor vehicle to be taken across an international border for a limited period.

Cascading Variance:

A sequential variance in which each deviation amplifies the previous deviation as result of uncorrected work.

Case Manager:

The individual assigned by an organization to be the single point of contact to the customer.

Case Study:

A complex and realistic exercise that offers practice using multiple skills, knowledge, and behaviors.

Cash Flow:

The actual monies flowing into or out of the business This may be different from the budget or profit/loss.

Catalyst:

A level of intervention that has the ability to accelerate the transition process.

Cause and Effect Diagram:

An analysis strategy that traces an undesirable effect back to the root cause.

Central Question:

A broad question posed by the researcher that asks for an exploration of the central concept in a study.

CEO Perspective:

A "big picture" view of the organization, its strengths and weaknesses, and the pressures for change.

Change (Breakthrough):

Groundbreaking organizational change, typically involving more than 50 percent performance improvement in key success dimensions.

Change (Culture):

The shift in the group sense of self.

Change (Incremental):

Minor organizational change, typically involving less than 10 percent performance improvement.

Change (Significant):

Moderate organizational change, typically involving 10 to 50 percent performance improvement.

Change Agent:

An individual charged with ensuring that the change takes place.

Change Control Board:

A group responsibility for reviewing, evaluating, approving, delaying, or rejecting changes to the project.

Change Control System:

A set of procedures that describes how modifications to the program are managed and controlled.

Change Control Tools:

Automated tools to assist with configuration management.

Change Drivers:

An internal or external pressure that shapes change to an organization.

Change Impact Assessment (CIA):

The starting point for developing your change plan so that you can actively manage the implications of your change project.

Change Log:

A list of all the changes recorded during a program.

Change Management:

The deliberate strategy of aligning organizational behaviors and/or attitudes.

Change Pressures:

Those internal or external factors that create a significant impact on organization for change.

Change Readiness Assessment (CRA):

An assessment that 'takes the temperature' of the organization throughout a project lifecycle, while focusing on people-related risks and readiness.

Change Request:

The skillsets, talents, and perspectives of people that are needed to complete/exceed the work.

Change Strategy:

A series of deliberate actions and processes designed to eliminate or reduce specific change pressures.

Channel Assembly:

In this model, the parts of the product are gathered and assembled as the product moves through the distribution channel.

Charter:

The overall purpose of the team or organization, including the mission, constraints, and sometimes the future vision.

Checklist Analysis:

A method for systematically evaluating resources using a list for completeness.

Chief Executive Officer (CEO):

The CEO serves as the face of the company and is the senior executive among the other C-suite members.

Chief Financial Officer (CFO):

The CFO position oversees an organization's financial operation. CFOs have global mindsets and work closely with CEOs to source new business opportunities while weighing the financial risks and benefits of each potential venture.

Chief Human Resources Officer (CHRO):

The CHRO position oversees an organization's personnel operation. This may include staffing, workforce planning, training, and organizational development.

Chief Information Officer (CIO):

The CIO is the person at an enterprise in charge of information technology (IT) strategy and the computer systems required to support the organization's unique objectives and goals. Sometimes referred to as Chief Technology Officer.

Chief Marketing Officer (CMO):

The CMO is an executive responsible for activities in an organization that have to do with creating, communicating and delivering offerings that have value for customers, clients or business partners.

Chief Operating Officer (COO):

The COO is an executive who oversees ongoing business operations within the company. The COO reports to the CEO and is usually second-in-command within the company.

Claim:

A request by a vendor against a buyer (or vice versa) for compensation under the terms of a contract.

Claims Administration:

The managing of communications, processes, and adjudication of a contract claim.

Classic Model:

A particular approach to organizing work based on the assumptions and principles of mass production.

Client:

A person or enterprise to whom your organization provides a service.

Close Project or Phase:

The finalizing of all work within a program or phase of a program.

Closing Process Group:

The group tasked with finalization of a program closer.

Coach:

A level of intervention that has the ability to accelerate the team development process.

Code of Accounts:

A numbering system used to identify each component of the work breakdown structure.

Code of Ethics:

The rules and principles drafted by professionals within a discipline.

Coding:

The process of organizing the material into chucks or segments of text and assigning a word or phrase to the segment in order to develop a general sense of it.

Collect Requirements:

A process to collect, document, and managing customer needs and requirements.

Colocation:

The strategic placement of program team members in the same physical space.

Command and Control:

An organizational structure and culture that supports a strict hierarchical distribution of power.

Commitment:

A firm administrative reservation of funds based upon firm procurement directives, orders, requisitions, authorizations to issue travel orders, or requests which authorize the recipient to create obligations without further recourse to the official responsible for certifying the availability of funds. The act of entering into a commitment is usually the first step in the process of spending available funds.

Common Experience:

An event or environment, simultaneously experienced by a team, group, or organization.

Common Impact:

A common experience, with significant individual impact, commonly shared by members of a team, group, or organization.

Common Service:

A sharable functionally that can used throughout an organization.

Communication:

The successful conveying or sharing of ideas, feelings, or information.

Communication Management Plan:

A plan that describes how to identify and account for program artifacts under configuration control.

Communication Requirements Analysis:

A process to identify the required individuals and/or work groups in a change effort throughout the transition.

Competencies:

The skills, knowledge and behaviors required for workers to perform business processes.

Conduct Procurements:

The process of obtaining vendor responses, selecting a vendor, an awarding a contract.

Confidence Interval:

An estimate in quantitative research of the range of upper and lower statistical values that are consistent with the observed data and are likely to contain the actual population mean.

Configuration:

Refers to all the components required to develop program success.

Configuration Management:

The ongoing process of identifying and managing changes to deliverables and other work products as they evolve through the program.

Configuration Management Plan:

A collection of procedures used to track, monitor, control changes to the program.

Confirmation Bias:

One of the longest-recognized and most pervasive forms of bias in research, confirmation bias occurs when a researcher forms a hypothesis or belief and uses respondents' information to confirm that belief.

Conformance:

A general concept of delivering results that fall within the limits that define acceptable variation for a quality requirement.

Consignment:

Agreement to pay a supplier of goods after the goods are sold.

Constraint:

The actions and tasks that creates a limitation or restriction.

Consultant:

A person who provides expert advice professionally.

Context:

The circumstances, environment, or setting of an action or concept.

Context Diagrams:

A visual depiction of the product scope showing a holistic business system.

Contextual Connection:

The context surrounding the communication or contact.

Contingency Plan:

An alternative strategy, typically including a series of actions designed to correct a problem situation.

Continuous Process Improvement (CPI):

The ongoing activities involved in improving quality of product/process.

Continuous Replenishment:

The idea of the continuous replenishment supply chain model is to constantly replenish the inventory by working closely with suppliers and/or intermediaries.

Contract:

A legally binding agreement between two entities documented in written form.

Contract Change Control System:

The system used to track, adjust, and communicate the changes of a contract.

Control (Project Management):

Comparing actual performance with planned performance and then making corrective actions as required.

Control Account:

A control approach in which scope, budget, actual cost, and schedule are integrated and compared to earned value for performance measurement.

Control Chart:

A qualitatively analytical process to reduce or eliminate process variances.

Control Costs:

The practice of identifying and reducing business expenses to increase profits, and it starts with the budgeting process.

Control Limits:

The horizontal lines drawn on a statistical process control chart, usually at a distance of ±3 standard deviations of the plotted statistic from the statistic's mean.

Control Procurements:

The process of managing supplier relationships, contract performance, and adjustments required for acquisition.

Control Quality:

The process of managing program requirements to meet customer needs.

Control Resources:

The process of managing program materiel, documentation, information, and personal for program success.

Control Schedule:

The process of managing program timelines and program work to meet program requirements.

Control Scope:

The process of managing the sum of all program requirements and program direct.

Controls:

The information that flow between the process and external control processes.

Corrective Action:

An action taken to adjust a program activity to align with program requirements.

Cost Account:

A control point at which actual costs are accumulated and compared to budgeted costs for the work performed.

Cost Aggregation:

Combining the total amount of the lower level program costs.

Cost Baseline:

The amount of money the project is predicted to cost.

Cost Management:

The process of planning and controlling the budget of a business.

Cost of Quality (CoQ):

The total amount of cost accrued to ensure customer standards are meet.

Cost Performance Index:

The measure of the financial effectiveness and efficiency of a project or program.

Cost Plus Award Fee Contract (CPAF):

A cost-reimbursement contract that provides for a fee consisting of (a) a base amount (which may be zero) fixed at inception of the contract and (b) an award amount, based upon a judgmental evaluation by the Government, sufficient to provide motivation for excellence in contract performance.

Cost Plus Fixed Fee Contract (CPFF):

A specific type of contract wherein the contractor is paid for the normal expenses for a project, plus an additional fixed fee for their services.

Cost Plus Incentive Fee Contract (CPIF):

A cost-reimbursement contract that provides for the initially negotiated fee to be adjusted later by a formula based on the relationship of total allowable costs to total target costs.

Cost Variance:

The amount of budget deficit or surplus expressed as the difference between the earned value and the actual cost.

Cost-Benefit Analysis:

A process business use to analyze decisions. The business or analyst sums the benefits of a situation or action and then subtracts the costs associated with taking that action.

Cost-Reimbursable Contract:

A contract where a contractor is paid for all of its allowed expenses to a set limit, plus additional payment to allow for a profit.

Crashing:

A project management approach where a schedule is shortened for the least cost by adding resources.

Creativity:

The process of creating something new and different.

Critical Success Factor (CSF):

An element that is necessary for an organization or project to achieve its mission.

Cross Docking:

A practice in logistics of unloading materials from an incoming semi-trailer truck or railroad car and loading these materials directly into outbound trucks, trailers, or rail cars, with little or no storage in between.

C-Suite (Executive):

The group of top senior staffers, which tend to start with the letter C, for "chief,". For example: CEO, CIO, CFO, or CHRO.

Cultural Foundation:

The underlying sense group identity of the overall organization.

Culture:

The acceptable norms, values, and beliefs within a group, organization, or society.

Culture Bias:

Assumptions about motivations and influences that are based on our cultural lens (on the spectrum of ethnocentricity or cultural relativity) create the culture bias. Ethnocentrism is judging another culture solely by the values and standards of one's own culture.

Customer:

Any individual organization whose inputs are your outputs.

Customer Needs:

The potential value or contribution of the product or service to the customer's processes.

Customer Set:

A group of customers distinguished by location, size, needs, values, or other characteristics and used for planning customer surveys within a business area.

Customer Values:

The success dimension that provide value-added to customers.

Customs:

The official department that administers and collects the duties levied by a government on imported goods.

CxO:

An acronym to describe a position among the executive level without using a specific position. The "x" is used to indicate a variable that could change depending on topic or context.

D.O.W.N.T.I.M.E.:

A lean six sigma acronym for the 8 forms of waste (defects, overproduction, waiting, not utilizing staff talent, travel, inventory, motion, excess processing).

Data Collection:

The process of gathering and measuring information on targeted variables in an established system, which then enables one to answer relevant questions and evaluate outcomes.

Decision Making:

The process of gathering and measuring information on targeted variables in an established system, which then enables one to answer relevant questions and evaluate outcomes.

Decision Tree Analysis:

A schematic representation of several decisions followed by different chances of the occurrence.

Decomposition:

A project management method used for dividing the scope and deliverables into more manageable parts.

Defect:

A shortcoming, imperfection, or lack.

Defect Repair:

An action to correct a nonconforming product or service.

Defense Transportation System:

The collection of transportation activities and carriers belonging to or under contract to the DoD. The DTS includes commercial and organic aircraft and ships, and commercial small package services under contract to the DoD, as well as the operation of U.S. military air and ocean terminals in and outside of the U.S.

Define Scope:

The series of actions required to detail the description of the program charter.

Define, Measure, Analyze, Improve and Control (DMA-IC):

A data-driven improvement cycle used for improving, optimizing and stabilizing business processes and designs.

Deliberation Analysis:

The study of organizational decision-making.

Deliver (SCOR):

The Deliver processes describe the activities associated with the creation, maintenance and fulfillment of customer orders.

Deliverable:

A work product given to the customer for acceptance.

Dependent Variable:

A variable whose value depends on that of another.

Deployment Phase:

The phase in which the program team puts the new business process into operation.

Deployment Site:

The geographical subdivision of a product release.

Descriptive Analysis:

An analysis of data for variables in a study that includes describing the results through means, standard deviation, and range of scores.

Descriptive Statistics:

A brief descriptive coefficient that summarize a given data set, which can be either a representation of the entire or a sample of a population.

Design of Experiments:

A systematic method to determine the relationship between factors affecting a process and the output of that process.

Development Approach:

The method used to create the product or service for the program life cycle.

Development Phase:

Creates or acquires the components of one release of a complete business solution.

Development Set:

A group of processes that are designed, built, and tested together using a conventional development approach.

Diagnostic Model:

A model that lists, summarizes, and evaluates current items specific to a model view.

Directing Unit:

It is a collection of business units brought together for a particular business purpose.

Direction Model:

A model that includes principles, constraints, assumptions, and standards related to a specific model view.

Directive Change Management (DCM):

A series of integrated impacts, deliberately taken, to align the actions and behaviors of all key stakeholders. The organizational leader typically defines the problem, communicates the problem, and sets strong consequences for success or failure.

DiSC:

The DiSC Index instrument uses the same self-report methodology that eliminates inter-rater reliability issues through the use of an objective scoring method. DiSC is an acronym for Dominance, Influencing, Submission, and Compliance.

Discrete Effort:

An action that can be planned that yields a specific output.

Discretionary Dependency:

A relationship that is established based on knowledge of best practices within a program where a specific sequence is desired.

Distributor:

An agent who supplies goods to stores and other businesses that sell to consumers.

DMADV:

A Six Sigma framework that focuses primarily on the development of a new service, product or process as opposed to improving a previously existing one.

Drop Shipment:

Delivery of merchandise from a manufacturer or original supplier direct to a buyer, without passing through the warehouse of a distributor or retailer (who generated and processed the sale). It is the most common form of fulfilling orders taken by most network marketing firms and internet-based retailers.

Duration:

The total number of time of work within a program or project.

Early Finish Date:

In the critical path method, it is the earliest possible completion date of work.

Early Start Date:

In the critical path method, it is the earliest possible beginning date of work.

Earned Value:

The calculated budget cost of work completed.

Earned Value Management:

A method to assess program performance of cost and schedule.

Economic Order Quantity (EOQ):

The most economical quantity of parts to order at one time to support a defined production rate, considering the applicable procurement and inventory costs.

Economic Sector:

A collection of customers with common industrial requirements, regulatory constraints, and business objectives.

Effectiveness:

Ability to produce an overall end-to-end product or process.

Efficiency:

Productivity and ability to produce a sub-product or sub-process (task or work cell).

Effort:

The use of resources, labor, and budget toward a common goal.

Electronic Data Interchange (EDI):

The transfer of data from one computer system to another by standardized message formatting, without the need for human intervention.

Elementary Business Process:

The lowest level component of structured activities within an organization.

Emotional Intelligence (EQ):

A term used to describe a complex ability to regulate your impulses, empathize with others, and persist and be resilient in the fac of obstacles.

Employee value:

The success dimension that provides value-added to employees.

Empowerment:

The level of self-authority and self-power.

Enable (SCOR):

The processes associated with establishing, maintaining and monitoring information, relationships, resources, assets, business rules, compliance and contracts required to operate the supply chain.

Enable (SCOR):

The processes associated with establishing, maintaining and monitoring information, relationships, resources, assets, business rules, compliance and contracts required to operate the supply chain.

End item:

A final combination of end products, component parts, and/or materials which is ready for its intended use, e.g., aircraft, ship, tank, mobile machine shop.

End of Life (EOL):

A term used with respect to a product supplied to customers, indicating that the product is in the end of its useful life (from the vendor's point of view), and a vendor stops marketing, selling, or rework sustaining it. (The vendor may simply intend to limit or end support for the product.)

End Product:

The final result of an activity or process.

Enterprise:

A Major organization with its own mission, goals, and performance objectives.

Enterprise Environmental Factors:

Conditions that influence a program not under control of the program manager.

Enterprise resource planning (ERP):

The ability to deliver an integrated suite of business applications. ERP tools share a common process and data model, covering broad and deep operational end-to-end processes, such as those found in finance, HR, distribution, manufacturing, service and the supply chain.

Entitlement:

Having or believing that a right benefits or privileges exists.

Entity:

A business unit or group important to the enterprise.

Essential Process:

The minimum set of required structured activities within an organization.

Estimate:

An assessment of the likely amount or outcome.

Estimate at Completion:

The expected cost at program completion.

Estimate Costs:

The expect amount of monetary expenses required for program success.

Estimate to Complete:

The expected cost required to complete a program in-process.

Ethnography:

A qualitative strategy in which the researcher studies the shared cultural patterns of a group in a natural setting over a prolonged period of time by collecting primarily observational and interview data.

Evaluation Criteria:

A benchmark, standard, or yardstick against which accomplishment, conformance, performance, and suitability of an individual, alternative, activity, product, or plan, as well as of risk-reward ratio is measured.

Event:

An occurrence that triggers the business to respond in a predictable fashion.

Execute:

To carry out or put into effect a plan, order, or course of action.

Experimental Design:

A test in quantitative research that examines the impact of an intervention on an outcome, controlling for all other factors that might influence that outcome.

Experimental Research:

A method to determine if a specific intervention influences an outcome in a study.

Expert Judgment:

An opinion provided based upon expertise in a functional area.

Explicit Knowledge:

Knowledge that can be codified using symbols, numbers, words, and/or pictures.

Extended Enterprise:

The expanding of process or program scope to include the processes of organizations external to the company.

External Actual Event:

An event initiated by a representative of an outside organization.

External Agent:

A person, group, or organization representing an outside source from your organization.

External Customer:

Individual or entity that is external to your organization whose process inputs are your process outputs.

External Dependency:

A relationship between program activities and non-program activities.

External Event:

An event that occurs outside the process thread.

External Result:

Results that goes beyond the immediate business area to affect its environment.

External Validity:

The validity of applying the conclusions of a research study outside the context of that study.

Facilitator:

A trained group dynamics expert that assist an organization understand their common objectives and assists them to plan how to achieve these objectives.

Fail Costs:

The cost incurred by a manufacturer when it produces defective goods.

Failure Modes and Effects Analysis (FMEA):

A structured approach to discovering potential failures that may exist within the design of a product or process.

Fast Tracking:

A schedule compression technique in which sequence are conducted in parallel.

Fee:

A payment made to a professional person or to a professional or public body in exchange for advice or services.

Feedback:

Information generated later in a process as a means to review and improve future processes.

Financial Flow:

The process structure of organizational assets conveyed in a monetary value.

Finish-to-Finish:

The relationship between two activities that prevents one activity from completion until the previous activity is complete.

Finish-to-Start:

The relationship between two activities that prevents one activity from starting until the previous activity is complete.

Firm Fixed Price Contract (FFP):

A contract provides for a price that is not subject to any adjustment on the basis of the contractor's cost experience in performing the contract.

First In, First Out (FIFO):

The oldest inventory items are recorded as sold first but do not necessarily mean that the exact oldest physical object has been tracked and sold.

First-run Yield:

The percentage of cases that go through the entire process thread the first time without any error or rework.

Fishbone Diagram:

A visualization tool for categorizing the potential causes of a problem in order to identify its root causes. (also called a cause and effect diagram).

Fixed Price Contract:

A type of contract where the payment amount does not depend on resources used or time expended.

Fixed Price Incentive Fee Contract (FPIF):

A type of contract that is able to offer contractors significant incentives when they take steps to control the costs of a project.

Fixed Price with Economic Price Adjustment Contract (FPEPA):

The amount of time that a task in a project network can be delayed without causing a delay to.

Float:

The amount of time that a task in a project network can be delayed without causing a delay to.

Flowchart:

A diagram that depicts a process, system or computer algorithm.

Focus Group:

A small, but demographically diverse group of people and whose reactions are studied especially in market research or political analysis in guided or open discussions about a new product or something else to determine the reactions that can be expected from a larger population.

Force Field Analysis:

A technique used to document the forces that enable or inhibit a particular change or a proposed action and to assess the relative impact of those forces.

Forecasting:

A technique that uses historical data as inputs to make informed estimates that are predictive in determining the direction of future trends.

Forward Pass:

A critical path method technique used to calculate the earliest start and finish dates from the program start date or a given point.

Fragmentation:

A dysfunctional division of labor that requires excessive time and effort to manage and coordinate separate workers in a process.

Freight Forwarder:

A commercial import/export company under contract to the customer who arranges transportation of materiel from a point specified to the final destination.

Freight on Board (FoB):

The point at which the costs and risks of shipped goods shift from the seller to the buyer.

Functional Area:

A major segment of business activity.

Funding Limit Reconciliation:

A comparison of the planned expenditures of program funds against any limits on the commitments of program funds to identify any variances.

Gage R&R (Repeatability and Reproducibility):

A methodology used to define the amount of variation in the measurement data due to the measurement system.

Gallup's StrengthsFinder:

A personality assessment with a focus on positive behaviors. This test measures what you do right. StrengthsFinder is aimed to identify a person's unique sequence of 34 themes of talent.

Gantt Chart:

A type of bar chart that illustrates a project schedule.

Gap Analysis:

A method of assessing the differences in performance between a business' information systems or software applications to determine whether business requirements are being met and, if not, what steps should be taken to ensure they are met successfully.

Gate:

An event marking a significant stage in development or project that MUST be completed prior to entering into the next stage of the development or project.

General Management Process:

A business process concerned with the overall performance of a business area, organizational unit, or performance indicator.

Goals:

The overall targets of an effort.

Grade:

A category used to itemize similar functions but do not share the same requirements for quality.

Green Belt:

A Six Sigma certification that demonstrates an individual's knowledge, skill, and ability to.

Ground Rules:

The expectations of individuals within a team or project.

Guiding principles:

A qualitative description of group-normalizing values and beliefs.

Habituation:

In cases of habituation bias, respondents provide the same answers to questions that are worded in similar ways.

Hard Allocation:

An allocation that has written to the stockm and stallocm table, this will prevent further hard allocations which cannot be fulfilled by the existing free stock.

Hardware:

All tools, machinery, and other durable equipment.

Hawthorne Effect:

The effect of productivity increase being directly related to managerial supervision and attention and then decreased in the absence of that attention.

Head Language:

Uses prose, words, and socially constructed artificial language. The language of management.

Heart Language:

Uses inflection, body language, 'natural' language. The language of leadership.

High Involvement Team (HIT):

A team that works to increase employee involvement significantly higher than the organizational norm.

High Performance Teams (HPT):

A work team that is able to improvement a single KPI by at least 50%.

High Performance Work System (HPWS):

An integrated system of HPTs.

Histogram:

A diagram consisting of rectangles whose area is proportional to the frequency of a variable and whose width is equal to the class interval.

Holding Cost:

Holding costs are those associated with storing inventory that remains unsold. These costs are one component of total inventory costs, along with ordering and shortage costs.

HPT Leader:

The person initially designed as the leader of an HPT effort.

Identity:

The distinct personality, makeup, and emotional processes of the individual.

Implementation:

The execution of plans to result in the desired outcomes.

Imposed Date:

The fixed date provided to program element. This date is normal expressed in a "No Later Than" format.

Incentive Fee:

A fee charged by a fund manager based on a fund's performance over a given period and usually compared to a benchmark.

Incremental Life Cycle:

A program life cycle that is iterative or incremental in which the deliverable is produced through a series of iterations that change form, fit, or function.

Independent Estimates:

An estimate obtained and analyzed from a neutral third party.

Independent Variable:

A variable whose variation does not depend on that of another.

Inferential Question:

A question that relates variable or compare group in terms of variables so that inferences can be drawn from the sample to the population.

Inferential Statistics:

Inferential statistics is one of the two main branches of statistics. Inferential statistics use a random sample of data taken from a population to describe and make inferences about the population.

Influence:

Exercised ability to shift others' actions/attitudes.

Influence Diagram:

A visual display of a decision problem. It depicts the key elements, including decisions, uncertainties, and objectives as nodes of various shapes and colors.

Information Flow:

Path data takes from its original setting to its end users.

Initiative:

A collection of interventions having a common theme.

Input:

The resources provided to the process by various suppliers. Inputs generally include facilities, equipment, labor, materials, services, information, or money.

Inspection:

The examination of work and/or the resulting deliverables.

Intangible:

Conceived and perceived without discrete sensory perception.

Integrated Make to Stock:

The integrated make-to-stock supply chain model focuses on tracking customer demand in real time, so that the production process can restock the finished goods inventory efficiently.

Integration Phase:

The phase in which the integration team brings together the individual components created or acquired separately during the Development Phase.

Integration plan:

An integration plan outlines exactly how and when major resources, assets, and processes of a company will be combined in order to achieve the goals of an effort.

Internal Actual Event:

An activity initiated either by some role player within the process thread or by a result of another process thread.

Internal Customer:

Individual or entity that is internal to your organization whose process inputs are your process outputs.

Internal Event:

An event that occurs inside the process thread.

Internal Result:

The outcome of an action. Internal results may go outside the process thread but will stay within the business area.

Internal Validity:

The approximate truth about inferences regarding cause-effect or causal relationships.

International Association for Six Sigma Certification (IASSC):

A professional association dedicated to growing and enhancing the standards within the Lean Six Sigma Community. IASSC is an independent third-party certification body.

Interpersonal Skills:

A term referring to an employee's ability to work well with others while performing their job. Interpersonal skills range from communication and listening to attitude and deportment. Sometimes referred to as "Soft Skills".

Interval (UoA):

A unit of analysis where the distance between attributes does have meaning. For example, when we measure temperature (in Fahrenheit), the distance from 30-40 is same as distance from 70-80.

Intervention:

Any action or strategy designed to preclude, divert, or accelerate an otherwise natural direction or outcome.

Interventions:

The tactics for bridging the gaps identified in a gap analysis.

Interview Protocol:

The process (or sequence) that a researcher will conduct an interview.

Inventory:

The term for merchandise or raw materials on hand.

Inventory Management:

The supervision of non-capitalized assets (inventory) and stock items.

Inventory Turnover:

A ratio showing how many times a company has sold and replaced inventory during a given period.

Invitation for Bid (IFB):

An invitation to contractors or equipment suppliers to bid on providing a specific project, product, and/or service.

Iteration:

The repetition until some expected testable condition is found.

Just-in-time (JIT):

A management strategy that aligns raw material orders from suppliers directly with production schedules.

Kaizen:

a Japanese term meaning "change for the better" or "continuous improvement.".

Kanban:

A manufacturing system in which the supply of components is regulated through the use of an instruction card sent along the production line.

Key Performance Indicator (KPI):

An essential value that demonstrates how effectively a company is achieving key business objectives.

Knowledge, Skills, & Abilities (KSA):

The knowledge, skills, and abilities that a person must possess in order to perform the duties of his or her position.

Lag:

The amount of time that an activity is delayed due to the previous activity.

Lagging Indicator:

A measurable performance factor that changes only after a business process has begun to follow a particular pattern or trend. A lagging indicator looks back at whether the intended result was achieved.

Landed Cost:

The total price of a product or shipment once it has arrived at a buyer's doorstep.

Last In, First Out (LIFO):

A cost flow assumption that can be used by U.S. companies in moving the costs of products from inventory to the cost of goods sold.

Late Finish Date:

A critical path method in which it provides the latest date that a task can finish without delaying the finish of the project.

Late Start Date:

A critical path method in which it provides the latest date that a task can start without delaying the finish of the project.

Lateral Thinking:

Diverging from normal patterns of perception to develop new methods, approaches, and ideas.

Lead Time:

The time between the initiation and completion of a production process.

Leader:

An individual that changes the natural speed and/or direction of an outcome.

Leading Indicator:

A measurable performance factor that changes before the performance metric begins to go in a particular direction. A leading indicator looks forward at future outcomes and events.

Leading Questions and Wording Bias:

Elaborating on a respondent's answer puts words in their mouth and, while leading questions and wording aren't types of bias themselves, they lead to bias or are a result of bias.

Lean Six Sigma:

A method that relies on a collaborative team effort to improve performance by systematically removing waste and reducing variation.

Lean Six Sigma Champion:

An individual assigned to a role by an organization to translate the company's vision, mission, goals and metrics to create an organizational deployment plan and identify individual projects.

Left-to-Right Thinking:

A mode of thinking about a process. It begins with the process, considers each step in the process, and makes an evaluation of process value and performance. It then designs improvements by identifying and fixing breakdowns and by streamlining the process.

Legacy System:

Any existing system developed prior to current technological industry standards.

Lessons Learned:

The knowledge gained during an effort that outlines improvements for future events.

Letter of Intent:

A document used during product acquisition to legally bind the company and vendor during the period between selecting the vendor and signing the contract.

Level of Effort:

An activity that does not produce a tangible product and is measured by time and schedule.

Leverage Points:

Any business processes potentially able to provide the greatest competitive advantage for business area.

Life Cycle (Business):

The progression of a process, program, project, or product over time. It is most commonly divided into five stages: launch, growth, shake-out, maturity, and decline.

Life Cycle Logistics:

A method to ensure sustainment considerations are integrated into all planning, implementation, management and oversight activities associated with the acquisition, development, production, fielding, support and disposal of a system across its life cycle.

Line of Sight:

A direct interface and interaction with a group or business area.

Linear Work:

The tasks, processes, and resources required to create a predefined product or service.

Linkage Diagram:

A visual map that identifies and categorizes relationships between organizational units.

Location Transparency:

The ability to use a resource without knowing its location.

Location Type:

A category used for a conceptual level analysis or design.

Logistics:

"The science of planning and carrying out the movement and maintenance of forces. In its most comprehensive sense, involves those aspects of supply chain operations which deal with:

A. Design and development, acquisition storage, movement, distribution, maintenance, evacuation, and disposition of materials.

B. Movement, evacuation, and hospitalization of personnel.

C. Acquisition or construction, maintenance, operation, and disposition of facilities.

D. Acquisitioning or furnishing of services".

Mainline Process Thread:
A process thread that is important and close to the heart of the business mission.

Major Process Thread:
Those few process threads that represent most of the work the enterprise does, the value it adds to its products, or its potential for improvement.

Make (SCOR):

The Make processes describe the activities associated with the conversion of materials or creation of the content for services.

Make-or-Buy Analysis:

The process of gathering and organizing data about product requirements and analyzing them against available alternatives including the purchase or internal manufacture of the product.

Management Reserve:

The amount of the total allocated budget withheld for management control purposes, rather than designated for the accomplishment of a specific task or set of tasks.

Manager:

An individual that's set priorities and allocates resources.

Mandatory Results:

A result necessarily produced by the process.

Manufacturer:

A person or company that makes goods for sale.

Manufacturing Resource Planning (MRP II):

A method for the effective planning of all resources of a manufacturing company.

Market:

In business, the term market refers to the group of consumers or organizations that is interested in the product, has the resources to purchase the product, and is permitted by law and other regulations to acquire the product.

Market Capitalization:

The total dollar market value of a company's outstanding shares. Commonly referred to as "market cap," it is calculated by multiplying a company's shares outstanding by the current market price of one share.

Market Share:

The portion of a market controlled by a particular company or product. Market share is calculated by taking the company's sales over the period and dividing it by the total sales of the industry over the same period.

Market Value:

The amount for which something can be sold on a given market.

Master Black Belt:

A Six Sigma certification that demonstrates an individual's knowledge, skill, and ability to train and coach Black Belts and Green Belts. Functions more at the Six Sigma program level by developing key metrics and the strategic direction. Acts as an organization's Six Sigma technologist and internal consultant.

Master Production Schedule (MPS):

A plan for individual commodities to be produced in each time period such as production, staffing, inventory, etc.

Master Schedule:

A schedule that identifies the major deliverables and work breakdown structure components and key milestone.

Material Requirements Planning (MRP I):

Computerized ordering and scheduling system for manufacturing and fabrication industries, it uses bill of materials data, inventory data, and master production schedule to project what material is required, when, and in what quantity.

Materials Management:

A core supply chain function and includes supply chain planning and supply chain execution capabilities. Specifically, materials management is the capability firms use to plan total material requirements.

Matrix Diagrams:

A table that allows sets of data to be compared in order to make better decisions.

Matrix Organization:

An individual that's set priorities and allocates resources.

Manager:

An organization in which there is dual or multiple managerial accountability and responsibility.

Mean:

The average is probably the most commonly used method of describing central tendency. To compute the mean all you do is add up all the values and divide by the number of values.

Mean Time Between Failures (MTBF):

The predicted elapsed time between inherent failures of a mechanical or electronic system, during normal system operation. MTBF can be calculated as the arithmetic mean (average) time between failures of a system.

Measurement System Analysis (MSA):

An experimental and mathematical method of determining how much the variation within the measurement process contributes to overall process variability.

Median:

The score found at the exact middle of the set of values. One way to compute the median is to list all scores in numerical order, and then locate the score in the center of the sample.

Mediating Variables:

Variables that "stand between" independent and dependent variables in a causal link.

Mentor:

Someone providing thought leadership and advice to the team without having routine interaction.

Method:

The collection and sequence of techniques used in an endeavor.

Metrics:

Regular measurements that can be analyzed.

Milestone:

An event marking a significant stage in development or project.

Mind Mapping:

A diagram used to visually organize information.

Minitab:

A statistical analysis software that automates calculations and the creation of graphs, allowing the user to focus more on the analysis of data and the interpretation of results.

Minor Process Threads:

Those do not represent significant work for the organization.

Mission (statement):

A short statement of the minimum requirements that an organization must achieve all the time to stay in business.

Mission Critical:

A make or break factor in the mission's success.

Mode:

The most frequently occurring value in the set of scores. To determine the mode, you might again order the scores as shown above, and then count each one. The most frequently occurring value is the mode.

Moderating Variables:

A variable that moderates the effect of independent variables in a study.

Module:

A logically self-contained and discrete part of a larger program.

Monte Carlo Simulation:

A technique used to understand the impact of risk and uncertainty in financial, project management, cost, and other forecasting models.

Muda:

A Japanese word meaning "futility; uselessness; wastefulness" and is a key concept in lean process thinking.

Mura:

a Japanese word meaning "unevenness; irregularity; lack of uniformity; nonuniformity; inequality" and is a key concept in lean process thinking.

Muri:

a Japanese word meaning "unreasonableness; impossible; beyond one's power; too difficult; by force; perforce; forcibly; compulsorily; excessiveness; immoderation" and is a key concept in lean process thinking.

Myers-Briggs Type Indicator (MBTI):

The Myers-Briggs Type Indicator assessment is a self-reported questionnaire designed to make Carl Jung's theory of personality types understandable and useful in everyday life. MBTI results identify valuable differences between normal, healthy people, difference that can be the source of much misunderstanding and miscommunication.

Object:

A thing to which a specified action or feeling is directed.

Objective:

A state the enterprise wishes to achieve en route to accomplishing its mission.

Obligation:

A duty to make a future payment of money. The duty is incurred as soon as an order is placed, or a contract is awarded for the delivery of goods and the performance of services. An obligation legally encumbers a specified sum of money which will require an outlay or expenditure in the future.

Observational Protocol:

The process (or sequence) that a researcher will record and observe an individual and/or group.

Obsolescence:

The process of becoming obsolete or outdated and no longer used.

Operation:

An action of a derived logical process, independent of the object addressed.

Operation Phase:

The phase that begins after the business processes and system have begun performing business functions.

Operational Excellence:

Providing customers with reliable products or services at competitive prices and delivering them with minimal difficulty and inconvenience.

Operational Value:

The success dimension that provides form/fit/function benefits of the product or service.

Opportunity:

A potential risk that may produce a positive effect on an objective.

Optional Result:

A result is not necessary to the process.

Ordinal (UoA):

A unit of analysis that the attributes can be rank ordered. The distances between attributes do not have any meaning. For example, on a survey you might code Educational Attainment as 0=less than high school; 1=some high school.; 2=high school degree; 3=some college; 4=college degree; 5=post college.

Organization:

A group of people associated for a particular purpose; generally, the overall enterprise.

Organization Infrastructure:

The systems, protocols, and processes that give structure to an organization, support its key functions, and embed routine practice.

Organization Support System:

The information technology infrastructure that establishes an environment for organizational and individual decision making.

Organizational Breakdown Structure:

A document that your business can use in conjunction with its workflow schedule and resource breakdown to organize the people who will be working on a particular project.

Organizational Change Management (OCM):

The alignment of the organization around Program/ Project success.

Organizational Chart:

A diagram outlining the positions or roles within the organization; typically includes reporting relationship.

Organizational Development:

The study of successful organizational change and performance.

Organizational Dimension:

The work force characteristics that play critical roles in business change.

Organizational Impact Assessment (OIA):

An evaluation to define who and where the greatest impact of a program onto an Organization will occur.

Organizational Learning:

The ability of an organization to learn from it experience.

Organizational Process Assets:

The plans, processes, policies, procedures, and knowledge bases specific to and used by the performing organization.

Organizational Readiness:

The level of desire for change, as applied to a specific change effort or outcome.

Organizational Resilience:

The ability of the organization to accept multiple changes; its adaptability and repeated acceptance of change.

Organizational Unit:

Any formally defined subset of an enterprise that exists for a specific business purpose.

Original Equipment Manufacturer (OEM):

A company that makes a final product for the consumer marketplace.

Other Tier Supplier:

Companies are the providers of basic raw materials.

Output:

The end product of a process.

Outsourcing:

The process of transferring work from internal resources (employees) to external resources (contractors).

Parametric Estimating:

A technique for estimating cost and duration, uses the relationship between variables to calculate the cost or duration.

Path Convergence:

A relationship in which a schedule activity has more than one predecessor.

Path Divergence:

A relationship in which a schedule activity has more than one successor.

Percent Complete:

The status of the duration of the task so far.

Perception:

The interpretation of sensory and environmental input.

Perform Integrated Change Control:

The process of reviewing all change requests; approving changes and managing changes to deliverables, organizational process assets, project documents, and the project management plan; and communicating their disposition.

Performance Engineering:

The process of modeling, estimating, or measuring the expected of actual resource consumption.

Performance Measurement:

The process of determining the value generated by the business process of the company.

Performance Measurement Baseline:

A time-phased resourced plan against which the accomplishment of authorized work can be measured.

Performance Reviews:

A formal assessment in which an evaluation is conducted regarding a project, program, and/or an employee's work performance. The intent of which is to identify strengths and weaknesses, offer feedback, and set goals for future performance.

Performance-Based Logistics (PBL):

The strategy of purchasing support in terms of systems readiness and performance outcome, rather than simply acquiring and stocking material on demand. An organization contracts with a manufacturer who is responsible for ensuring optimum system performance by providing complete logistics support to the customer.

Perspective:

A subjective evaluation of objects or events of relative significance.

Phase:

A discrete stage of development.

Phase Gate:

An event marking the end of a project stage that MUST be completed prior to entering into the next stage of the project.

Phenomenology:

A research method that explores and ascribes the essences of human experiences as it relates to the phenomenon being studied.

Physical Flow:

The process of the movement of goods from a supplier to a customer, as well as any customer returns or service needs.

Pilot Site:

The physical location in which a pre-launched product, service, or process is tested.

Plan (SCOR):

The Plan processes describe the activities associated with developing plans to operate the supply chain.

Planned Value:

The approved value of the work to be completed in a given time.

Planning Package:

A logical aggregation of future work within a control account that cannot yet be planned in detail at the work package or task level.

Plurality:

Decisions made by the largest subsect group.

Point of Use Inventory:

This is a lean manufacturing practice that tends to minimize the amount of inventory kept on hand since available space is typically limited at the point-of-use.

Poka Yoke:

A Japanese term that means "mistake-proofing" or "inadvertent error prevention".

Policy:

A deliberate system of principles to guide decisions and achieve rational outcomes.

Polymorphism:

A situation in which behavior of an operation varies depending on the class of object performing the operation.

Population (Research):

A large collection of individuals or objects that is the main focus of a scientific query.

Portfolio:

A compilation of materials that exemplifies your beliefs, skills, qualifications, education, training and experiences.

Power (Organizational):

Inherent ability to shift others' action/attitudes via own actions/attitudes.

Precedence Diagramming Method:

A visual representation technique that depicts the activities involved in a project.

Precision:

The average attempt is not on the center of the target, but the variability is small.

Predecessor Activity:

An activity that precedes another activity – not in the chronological sense but according to their dependency to each other.

Predictive Life Cycle:

The cycles in which the scope, deadline and cost are determined as soon as possible in the program life cycle and efforts are focused on meeting the commitments established for each one of these factors.

Predictive Modeling:

A process that uses data mining and probability to forecast outcomes.

Prevention Costs:

The costs incurred to avoid or minimize the number of program or product defects.

Preventive Action:

A change implemented to address a weakness in a management system that is not yet responsible for causing nonconforming product or service.

Primary Process Group:

A set of closely related activities responding to one or more related events and producing one or more defined result.

Primary Result:

The process thread's main response to an event.

Prioritization Matrix:

A tool used to create a set of criteria and use them to rate a program.

Probability and Impact Matrix:

A tool used to determine which risks need detailed risk response plans.

Procedure:

A series of actions conducted in a certain order or manner.

Process:

An activity with clear starting and stopping points.

Process Decomposition:

A technique of successively dividing processes. The work of any enterprise or business area can be broken into processes. These processes can be divided further into subprocesses, which in turn can be divided.

Process Dynamics Modeling:

The design of several detailed levels of process flow.

Process Enablement:

To reduce or eliminate duplication of information, wasting time looking for the information, bottlenecks, and errors caused by using outdated information while achieving the goal of the process.

Process Flow:

The logic sequence among the business process.

Process Map:

A planning and management tool that visually describes the flow of work.

Process Scenario:

A description of what a vendor should demonstrate about how a product supports an elementary business process.

Process Thread:

A set of activities the enterprise performs in response to a single event.

Procurement Audits:

A process that reviews different contracts and contracting processes to determine the completeness, efficacy as well as the accuracy of the procurement process.

Product:

Any tangible item, intangible item, or service provided to a customer.

Product Analysis:

A tool used to define scope that generally means asking questions about a product and forming answers to describe the use, characteristics, and other relevant aspects of what is going to be built or manufactured.

Product Cycle Times:

The period it takes for a manufacturer to complete development and production of a new or modified product.

Product Leadership:

Changing the natural speed and/or direction of a product life cycle.

Product life cycle:

The normal process of product market development broken into four stages: introduction, growth, maturity, and decline.

Product Scope:

The features and functions that characterize a product, service, or result.

Production Lead Time:

The manufacturing lead time is the time period between the placement of an order and the shipment of the completed order to the customer.

Productivity:

Ability to produce product/process measured against time/resource/acceptance.

Program:

A plan of action aimed at accomplishing a clear business objective, with details on what work is to be done, by whom, when, and what means, or resources will be used.

Programme:

A collection of projects related to a common strategic objective.

Programme Management:

The maintaining of a strategic perspective to ensure that the projects within a programme align with the goals and business strategy.

Project:

A related group of tasks organized under the direction of a manager for the purpose of achieving a specified result.

Project Calendar:

The particular calendar in which the program is outlined and or delineated via a few specific mechanisms.

Project Charter:

A formal, typically short document that describes your project in its entirety — including what the objectives are, how it will be carried out, and who the stakeholders are.

Project Governance:

The framework, functions, and processes that guide program management activities in order to meet operational goals.

Project Initiation:

The 1st phase in the Project Management Life Cycle, as it involves starting up a new project.

Project Management:

The practice of initiating, planning, executing, controlling, and closing the work of a team to achieve specific goals and meet specific success criteria at the specified time.

Project Management Body of Knowledge (PMBOK):

A set of standard terminology and guidelines (a body of knowledge) for project management.

Project Management Office (PMO):

A group or department within a business, government agency, or enterprise that defines and maintains standards for project management within the organization.

Project Manager:

The individual assigned by an organization to hold the responsibility of the planning, procurement and execution of a project, in any undertaking that has a defined scope, defined start and a defined finish; regardless of industry.

Project Phase:

A collection of logically related project activities that culminates in the completion of deliverables.

Project Scope:

The part of project planning that involves determining and documenting a list of specific project goals, deliverables, features, functions, tasks, deadlines, and ultimately costs.

Pull System of Inventory Control:

The pull inventory control system begins with a customer's order. With this strategy, companies only make enough product to fulfill customer's orders.

Push System of Inventory Control:

The push system of inventory control involves forecasting inventory needs to meet customer demand. The company will in turn produce enough product to meet the forecast demand and sell, or push, the goods to the consumer.

Qualitative Research:

An approach to research that attempts to explore and understand the meaning individuals or groups ascribe to a social or human problem.

Quality:

Conformity to a group of products/processes or to an external standard.

Quality Control Costs:

The total cost of quality-related efforts to prevent and/or mitigate deficiencies.

Quality Report:

A document that records quality management issues, corrective actions, and potential quality control actions for program improvement.

Quantitative Research:

A means for testing objective theories by examining the relationship among variables.

Quasi-Experiment:

A form of experimental research in which individuals are not randomly assigned to groups.

Question-order bias:

One question can influence answers to subsequent questions, creating question-order bias.

Quick Hits:

Potential short-duration, low risk projects.

RACI Chart:

A matrix of all the activities or decision-making authorities undertaken in an organization set against all the people or roles. At each intersection of activity and role it is possible to assign somebody responsible, accountable, consulted or informed for that activity or decision.

Ratio (UoA):

A unit of analysis where the measurement is always an absolute zero that is meaningful. This means that you can construct a meaningful fraction (or ratio) with a ratio variable. Weight is a ratio variable.

Raw Material:

The basic material from which a product is made.

Recognition:

Any non-monetary reinforcement.

Re-Engineering:

The study of evaluating business and enterprise process described has no variances and no workarounds.

Reflexivity:

A research method in which the researcher reflects about how their biases, values, and personal background shaped their interpretations of the data within a study.

Regression Analysis:

A statistical method that allows you to examine the relationship between two or more variables of interest. Typically, the influence of one or more independent variables on a dependent variable.

Relationship:

The connections or business rules that exist between entities.

Reliability:

In research, it refers to whether scores to items on an instrument are internally consistent, stable over time, and whether there was consistency in test administration and scoring.

Reorder Point:

The level of inventory which triggers an action to replenish that particular inventory stock.

Repair of Repairables (RoR):

An item that can be reconditioned or economically repaired for reuse when it becomes unserviceable.

Repairable Item Replacement Option (RIRO):

A method that allows a customer to replace unserviceable depot level repairable items instead of repairing them.

Repeatability:

The closeness of the agreement between the results of successive measurements of the same measure carried out under the same conditions of measurement.

Reproductibility:

The ability to be reproduced or copied. In research, it measures whether an entire study or experiment can be reproduced in its entirety.

Request for Information (RFI):

A standard business process whose purpose is to collect written information about the capabilities of various suppliers.

Request for Proposal (RFP):

A document that solicits proposal, often made through a bidding process, by an agency or company interested in procurement of a commodity, service, or valuable asset, to potential suppliers to submit business proposals.

Request for Quotation (RFQ):

A document that an organization submits to one or more potential suppliers eliciting quotations for a product or service. Typically, an RFQ seeks an itemized list of prices for something that is well-defined and quantifiable.

Request for Solution (RFS):

A procurement document inviting vendors to participate in the process of developing a solution to a set of clearly defined business problems.

Requirement (Project Management):

The expectation of program stakeholders on program outcomes.

Requirements Traceability Matrix:

A tool to help ensure that the program's scope, requirements, and deliverables remain "as is" when compared to the baseline. It tracks the deliverables by establishing a thread for each requirement- from the program's initiation to the final implementation.

Research Approach:

The plans and the procedures for research that span the decisions from a broad assumption to detailed methods of data collection and analysis.

Research Bias:

A process where the scientists performing the research influence the results, in order to portray a certain outcome.

Research Designs:

The type of inquiry within research that provides specific direction for procedures in a research study.

Research Methods:

The form of data collection, analysis, and interpretation that researchers propose for their studies.

Resource Allocation:

The process of assigning and managing assets in a manner that supports an organization's strategic goals.

Resource Breakdown Structure:

A hierarchical list of resources related by function and resource type that is used to facilitate planning and controlling of project work.

Resource Leveling:

A technique in project management that overlooks resource allocation and resolves possible conflict arising from over-allocation.

Respondent Bias:

Any error in a study that is a result of participants' inability or unwillingness to provide accurate or honest answers to a survey.

Responsibility (Project Management):

An assignment that can be delegated within a plan such that the assigned resources incurs a duty to perform the requirements of the assignment.

Responsibility Assignment Matrix:

A description of the participation by various roles in completing tasks or deliverables for a project or business process.

Result:

An output of an activity or process.

Return (SCOR):

The Return processes describe the activities associated with the reverse flow of goods.

Return on Assets (ROA):

Financial calculation indicating the payback of any given investment or capital good.

Return on Investment (ROI):

A performance measure used to evaluate the efficiency of an investment or compare the efficiency of a number of different investments.

Reverse Auction:

A type of auction in which sellers bid for the prices at which they are willing to sell their goods and services.

Reverse Flow Logistics:

It is "the process of moving goods from their typical final destination for the purpose of capturing value, or proper disposal.

Reward:

Monetary reinforcement.

Right-to-Left Thinking:

A mode of thinking about a process. It begins with the outputs, considers their value and then evaluates or defines the total process to deliver those outputs.

Risk:

An uncertain event that may impact one or more objectives; to which the positive or negative impact is unknown.

Risk Assessment:

A process to identify potential hazards and analyze what could happen if a hazard occurs.

Risk Breakdown Structure:

A hierarchical representation of risks according to their risk categories.

Risk Categorization:

The organization of risks based on their sources, areas of the affected project and other useful categories in order to determine the areas of the project that are the most exposed to the effects of risks or uncertainties.

Risk Escalation:

A risk management process whereby an increasingly higher level of authorization is required to sanction the continued tolerance of increasingly higher levels of risk.

Risk Exploiting:

A risk response strategy whereby the project team acts to ensure that an opportunity occurs.

Risk Exposure:

The measure of potential future loss resulting from a specific activity or event.

Risk Mitigation:

The taken to eliminate, reduce, or control project risks.

Risk Mitigation Strategy:

A set of actions directed at minimizing the potential negative impacts of risk a program's success.

Risk Report:

A document developed throughout a program which outlines the program's risk.

Role:

A function performed by an individual and his/her/zhe corresponding duties.

Root Cause Analysis:

A systematic process for identifying "root causes" of problems or events and an approach for responding to them.

Safety Stock:

The quantity of materiel, in addition to the operating level of supply required to be on hand to permit continuous operations.

Sample (Research):

A group of people, objects, or items that are taken from a larger population for measurement.

Sandbox:

A listing of constraints typically performed by an individual with the HPT goals.

Scalability:

The capacity to be changed in size or scale.

Schedule Performance Index:

A measure of how close the project is to being completed compared to the schedule.

Schedule Variance:

An indicator of whether a project schedule is ahead or behind and is typically used within Earned Value Management (EVM). Schedule Variance can be calculated by subtracting the Budgeted Cost of Work Scheduled (BCWS) from the Budgeted Cost of Work Performed (BCWP).

Scientific Management:

A theory of management that analyzes and synthesizes workflows.

Scope:

The sum of the products, services, and results to be provided as a program.

Scope Baseline:

A part of the project management plan and acts as the reference point through the project life.

Script Case:

A way of demonstrating a major process thread.

Scrum:

A framework that helps teams work together. Scrum encourages teams to learn through experiences, self-organize while working on a problem, and reflect on their wins and losses to continuously improve.

Secondary Result:

A result occurring in addition to the primary result of the process thread.

Secondary Risk:

A risk created by the response to another risk.

Self-Organizing Teams:

A team that determines for themselves how best to accomplish their work, rather than being directed by others outside the team.

Seller:

A provider or supplier of products, services, or results to an organization.

Sensitivity Analysis:

The study of how the uncertainty in the output of a mathematical model or system (numerical or otherwise) can be divided and allocated to different sources of uncertainty in its inputs.

Serializable:

The effect of a set of transactions is as if they executed one after the other, even though they may execute concurrently.

Servant Leadership:

A leadership philosophy in which an individual interacts with others, either in a management or fellow employee capacity, with the aim of achieving authority rather than power.

Service:

The provision of unique actions or benefits that provide value in and of themselves.

Service Level Agreements:

A commitment between a service provider and a client. Particular aspects of the service (quality, availability, responsibilities) are agreed between the service provider and the service user.

Set in order (5S):

To neatly arrange and identify parts and tools for ease of use.

Shelf Life:

The length of time for which an item remains usable, fit for consumption, or saleable.

Shine (5S):

To conduct a cleanup campaign.

Sigma (statistical):

A symbol for the standard from the ideal process.

SIPOC:

A tool that summarizes the inputs and outputs of one or more processes in table form. The acronym SIPOC stands for suppliers, inputs, process, outputs, and customers.

Situational Leader:

A leader that adjusts their leadership methods depending on the context of the situation.

Six Sigma (statistical):

A process having no more than 3.4 defect/problem per 1 million opportunities.

Small Medium Business (SMB):

A business with 100 or fewer employees is generally considered small, while one with 100-999 employees is considered to be medium-sized.

Social Desirability Bias:

This bias involves respondents answering questions in a way that they think will lead to being accepted and liked.

Soft Allocation:

A quantity of an inventory item that is reserved for use in a specific warehouse operation.

Sort (5S):

To separate needed tools, parts, and instructions from unneeded materials and to remove the unneeded ones.

Soul Language:

Uses symbols, unconscious, different forms of consciousness to communicate. The language of gnosis and communitas.

Source (SCOR):

The Source processes describe the ordering (or scheduling of deliveries) and receipt of goods and services.

Source Selection Criteria:

A set of attributes desired by the buyer which a seller is required to meet or exceed to be selected for a contract.

Sourcing:

The process of finding suppliers of goods or services.

Spaghetti Diagram:

A visual representation of the actual path taken by people as they move through a process within a department to complete their jobs.

Specialty Area:

An area of specific interest in which an individual, group, or organization have become an expert.

Specification:

A set of documented requirements to be satisfied by a material, design, product, or service.

Sponsor:

A person or group who provides resources and support for a program.

Sponsor bias:

When respondents know – or suspect – the sponsor of the research, their feelings and opinions about that sponsor may bias their answers. Respondents' views on the sponsoring organization's mission or core beliefs, for example, can influence how they answer all questions related to that brand.

Staging:

Refers to a process of storing goods before shipment in supply chain management. The designated area is known as 'staging area'. Hence, staging area is the space used for interim storage only and should be located in proximity to the shipment area assigned to them.

Stakeholder:

A person with an interest or concern in something.

Standard Deviation:

A quantity calculated to indicate the extent of deviation for a group as a whole.

Standard Operating Procedure (SOP):

A set of step-by-step instructions compiled by an organization to help workers carry out complex routine operations. SOPs aim to achieve efficiency, quality output and uniformity of performance, while reducing miscommunication and failure to comply with industry regulations.

Standardize (5S):

To conduct "sort", "set in order", and "shine" daily to maintain a workplace in perfect condition.

Start Date:

The calendar day on which a project initiates.

Start-to-Finish:

The relationship in which a successor activity cannot finish until a predecessor activity has started.

Start-to-Start:

The relationship in which a successor activity cannot start until a predecessor activity has started.

Statement of Work:

A document that defines the description of a project's work requirement. It defines project-specific activities, deliverables and timelines for a vendor providing services to the client.

Statistical Package for the Social Sciences (SPSS):

A software package used for interactive, or batched, statistical analysis.

Statistical Process Control (SPC):

A set of procedures and quality tools help monitor process behavior & find solutions for production issues.

Statistical Quality Management:

The use of statistical methods in the monitoring and maintaining of the quality of products and services.

Status quo:

The present or existing state.

Strategic:

A method or plan chosen to bring about a desired future, such as achievement of a goal or solution to a problem.

Strategic Thinking:

A perspective that envisions new innovations and futures. A way of seeing the Big Picture that focuses on interconnectedness.

Strategy:

A general approach to move forward that incorporates people and forces outside of your 'local group' and looks into the future to support unique/perceived/value added.

Structure:

An individual that set tasks for their workgroup.

Subject Matter Expert (SME):

One who provides particular expertise on a given subject.

Subphase:

A subsection of a phase.

Subtype:

A lower level subclassification of an entity within a higher-level type.

Success Dimension:

Key business success dimensions include customer value employee value, operational value, shareholder value, and cultural foundation.

Supertype:

A higher-level grouping or abstraction of one or more entities.

Supervisor:

Someone responsible for the work to be done, typically at the task level.

Supplier:

A person or organization that provides something needed such as a product or service.

Supply Chain:

The sequence of processes involved in the production and distribution of a commodity.

Supply Chain Management:

The active management of supply chain activities to maximize customer value and achieve a sustainable competitive advantage.

Supply Chain Operations Reference (SCOR):

A process reference model developed and endorsed by the Supply Chain Council as the cross-industry, standard diagnostic tool for supply chain management.

Supply Discrepancy Report (SDR):

A process for customers to file a complaint with an organization for product loss, quality deficiencies, damage, and various other problems associated with the delivery of material.

Support Process:

A process whose sole purpose is to help bridge the gap between the current and future states of an organization.

Surrogate:

An artificial construct established to represent a class of elementary business processes.

Sustain (5S):

To form the habit of always following the first four S's.

SWOT Analysis:

An analysis that provides a visual chart in which to make a rational choice based on a subject's strengths, weaknesses, opportunities, and threats.

SWOT Identification:

A strategic planning technique used to help a person or organization identify strengths, weaknesses, opportunities, and threats related to business competition or project planning.

System:

A collection of interdependent manual and automated processes with a supporting infrastructure, facilities, and organization working together to produce a business result.

Tacit Knowledge:

The kind of knowledge that is difficult to transfer to another person by means of writing it down or verbalizing it.

Takt Time:

The average time between the start of production of one unit and the start of production of the next unit, when these production starts are set to match the rate of customer demand.

Tangible:

Having a discrete boundary, typically discernible by physical senses.

Task:

A coherent of work that can be assigned to an individual or small and completed in a reasonable period of time.

Team:

An interdependent work group comprised of people who share a common goal.

Template:

A pattern used as a guide for producing a product or service.

Test Case:

A unique path of a business transaction through a set of processes.

Test Category:

A collection of test types performed at a specific point in the overall development process.

Test Type:

A specific type of testing aimed at verifying one aspect of organizational change.

The Halo Effect:

Moderators and respondents have a tendency to see something or someone in a certain light because of a single, positive attribute.

Thematic Analysis:

A method for identifying, analyzing and reporting patterns (themes) within data.

Theme:

An idea that captures something important about the data in relation to the research question that represents a pattern in responses.

Theory of Constraints (ToC):

A management paradigm that views any manageable system as being limited in achieving more of its goals by a very small number of constraints.

Third Party Transfer:

The transfer of materials, services, and/or training to an organization (a third company or individual) from a company that originally acquired such items. As a condition of the original sale or transfer, the recipient organization must obtain the consent of the original organization (OEM) for any proposed third-party transfer.

Thought Leadership:

Providing unique ideas and conceptual guidance for a given process or effort.

Threat (Project Management):

A risk that may have a negative effect on the organizational goal.

Threshold:

A predetermined program limit value that dictates action to be taken if limit is reached.

Tier:

A level or grade within the hierarchy of an organization or system.

Tier One Supplier:

Tier one companies are direct suppliers to OEMs.

Tier Two Supplier:

Tier two companies are the key suppliers to tier one suppliers, without supplying a product directly to OEM companies.

Time and Material Contract:

An arrangement under which a contractor is paid on the basis of actual cost of direct labor, materials and equipment usage, and fixed contractor's overheads.

Time Efficiency:

The elapsed time consumed per transaction, batch, or other unit of production.

Time Series:

A series of data points indexed (or listed or graphed) in time order.

To-Be:

The future state.

To-Complete Performance Index:

A comparative Earn Value Management metric used primarily to determine if an independent estimate at completion is reasonable.

Tolerance:

Allowable departure from a specification or standard, considered non-harmful to the functioning of a part, process, or product over its life cycle.

Topic:

The subject of a proposed study identified by a researcher.

Tornado Diagram:

A tool used to depict the sensitivity of a result to changes in selected variables.

Total Cost of Ownership:

The purchase price of an asset plus the costs of operation. Assessing the total cost of ownership represents taking a bigger picture look at what the product is and what its value is over time.

Total Float:

The amount of time that an activity can be delayed from its early start date without delaying the project finish date.

Total Production Cost:

Total-absorbed-cost to produce end-to-end product/process.

Total Quality Costs:

All costs accrued related to of quality-related efforts and deficiencies.

Total Quality Management (TQM):

A structured approach to overall organizational management. The focus of the process is to improve the quality of an organization's outputs, including goods and services, through continual improvement of internal practices.

Touch Time:

The time that the product is actually being worked on, and value is being added.

Toyota Production System (TPS):

An integrated socio-technical system developed by Toyota (automotive manufacturer) to efficiently organize manufacturing and logistics, including the interaction with suppliers and customers, to minimize cost and waste.

Training Plan:

A strategy to provide necessary skilling for all key stakeholders required to achieve success.

Transactional Leader:

A leader that offers a series of rewards or punishment to the people within their group in exchange for task completion or project support.

Transcendence Teams:

A work team that is able to simultaneously improvement all KPIs by at least 50%.

Transformational Leader:

A leader that inspires their organization through the translation of the organizational vision to the members within that organization as the vision relate to them.

Transition:

The process of changing from one state or phase to another.

Transition Plan:

A deliberate plan to transition from As-Is to the To-Be; typically, comprehensive and detailed.

Transportation:

The action of transporting someone or something or the process of being transported.

Transshipment:

The shipment of goods or containers to an intermediate destination, then to another destination.

Trend Analysis:

A statistical technique that tries to determine future movements of a given variable by analyzing historical trends.

Trigger Condition:

An event that indicates that a risk is about to occur.

Trustworthiness:

The validation of data in qualitative research. This is often conducted through the triangularization of information from multiple sources to verify the results of a study.

Uniform Materiel Movement and Issue Priority System (UMMIPS):

A system of ranking materiel requirements and time standards for requisition processing and materiel movement through the use of a two-digit priority designator. It identifies the relative importance of competing demands for logistics resources.

Unique/ Perceived/Value-Add:

The concept of offering a one of a kind, positive benefit in a success dimension as interpreted by an external entity.

Unit of Analysis (UoA):

The most elementary part of the phenomenon to be studied; its character influences research design, data collection, and data analysis decisions.

Validate Scope:

The process of formalizing acceptance of the completed project deliverables.

Validation:

The action of checking or proving the validity or accuracy of something.

Value Added:

Providing a positive benefit in a success dimension.

Value Added Resaler (VAR):

A company that adds features or services to an existing product, then resells it (usually to end-users) as an integrated product or complete "turn-key" solution.

Value Added Tax (VAT):

A tax on the amount by which the value of an article has been increased at each stage of its production or distribution.

Value Chain:

The collection of activities performed to develop, produce, market, and deliver products and services to customers.

Value Discipline:

Any one of the three potential sets of values favored by customers and emphasized by companies in their business strategies: customer intimacy, operational excellence, and product leadership.

Value Stream:

Artifacts within business architecture that allow a business to specify the value proposition derived by an external (e.g., customer) or internal stakeholder from an organization.

Value-Stream Analysis:

The analytical process that separates those activities that contribute to value creation from activities that create waste and identifies opportunities for improvement.

Value-Stream Map:

A lean management tool that helps visualize the steps needed to take from product creation to delivering it to the end-customer.

Variable:

A variable is any entity that can take on different values. OK, so what does that mean? Anything that can vary can be considered a variable.

Variance:

Any deviation from the expected performance of a process or the natural flow of work.

Variance at Completion:

The projected amount of difference between the original budget estimate at completion and the projected budget estimate.

Verification:

The process of establishing the truth, accuracy, or validity of something.

Virtual Corporation:

A company that dynamically creates temporary alliances with its suppliers and customers to pursue particular opportunities.

Virtual Team:

A group of individuals who work together from different geographic locations and rely on communication technology such as email, FAX, and video or voice conferencing services in order to collaborate.

Visibility:

The ability of parts, components or products in transit to be tracked from the manufacturer to their final destination.

Vision (Statement):

A short statement the aims and values of an organization.

Vision and Strategy Phase:

The phase in which business change is addressed on an enterprise-wide basis.

Voice of the Customer (VoC):

A term used to describe the in-depth process of capturing customer's expectations, preferences and aversions.

Walkthrough:

A structured examination of a design or process with the intention of discovering errors and improvement opportunities.

Waterfall Approach:

A project management approach where a project is completed in distinct stages and moved in a linear step by step stages until project completion.

Waybill:

A list of passengers or goods being carried on a vehicle.

White Belt:

A Six Sigma certification that demonstrates an understanding of basic Six Sigma concepts from an awareness perspective.

Work:

The overall effort directed toward the creation of a service or product.

Work Breakdown Structure:

A deliverable-oriented breakdown of a project into smaller components.

Work Force Structure:

The formal reporting lines and informal work group structures.

Work Group:

A collection of individual working together in roles coordinated to achieve common objectives.

Work Group Structure:

A structure that describes the relationships between roles included within a single work group.

Work in Progress (WIP):

A production and supply-chain management term describing partially finished goods awaiting completion. WIP refers to the raw materials, labor, and overhead costs incurred for products that are at various stages of the production process.

Work Package:

The work defined at the lowest level of the work breakdown structure.

Work Product:

The tangible result of one or more tasks.

Work Sessions:

Similar to workshops but generally smaller and less formal.

Workshop:

Formal meetings for six to sixteen participants that may last from one to several days. Designed to inspire a positive, collaborative environment, workshops precipitate early, collective user involvement in and ownership of a project.

Yellow Belt:

A Six Sigma certification that demonstrates an individual's knowledge, skill, and ability to participate as a project team member. Reviews process improvements that support the project.